**FUN 轻松学
美国各学科**

阅读课本 **1**

Preschool
动词篇

【美】普特莱克　【韩】韩国逸创文化 ●著
欧宝妮 ●译

江苏科学技术出版社　凤凰含章

图书在版编目（CIP）数据

　　轻松学美国各学科阅读课本 . 1, 动词篇 / 美国普特
莱克 , 韩国逸创文化著 ; 欧宝妮译 . -- 南京 : 江苏科
学技术出版社 , 2014.6
　　（易人外语）
　　ISBN 978-7-5537-3062-2

　　Ⅰ . ①轻… Ⅱ . ①美… ②韩… ③欧… Ⅲ . ①英语 –
动词 – 学前教育 – 教学参考资料 Ⅳ . ① G613.2

　　中国版本图书馆 CIP 数据核字 (2014) 第 072759 号

미국교과서 읽는 리딩 Reading key Preschool 예비과정편 1
Copyright © 2012 by Key Publications
All rights reserved
Simplified Chinese copyright © 2014 by Phoenix-HanZhang Publishing
and Media (Tianjin) Co., Ltd.
This Simplified Chinese edition was published by arrangement with Key
Publications through Agency Liang

译本授权：寂天文化事业有限公司

江苏省版权局著作权合同登记 图字：10-2014-183 号

轻松学美国各学科 阅读课本 1（动词篇）

著　　　者	【美】普特莱克【韩】韩国逸创文化
译　　　者	欧宝妮
责 任 编 辑	樊　明　葛　昀
责 任 监 制	曹叶平　周雅婷

出 版 发 行	凤凰出版传媒股份有限公司 江苏科学技术出版社
出版社地址	南京市湖南路 1 号 A 楼，邮编：210009
出版社网址	http://www.pspress.cn
经　　　销	凤凰出版传媒股份有限公司
印　　　刷	北京旭丰源印刷技术有限公司

开　　　本	787 mm × 1092 mm　　1/16
印　　　张	10
字　　　数	130 千字
版　　　次	2014 年 6 月第 1 版
印　　　次	2014 年 6 月第 1 次印刷

标 准 书 号	ISBN 978-7-5537-3062-2
定　　　价	32.00 元（含光盘）

图书如有印装质量问题，可随时向我社出版科调换。

The Best Preparation for Building Basic Vocabulary and Grammar

The Reading Key – Preschool series is designed to help children understand basic words and grammar to learn English. This series also helps children develop their reading skills in a fun and easy way.

Features

- Learning high-frequency words that appear in all kinds of reading materials
- Building basic grammar and reading comprehension skills to learn English
- Various activities including reading and writing practice
- A wide variety of topics that cover American school subjects
- Full-color photographs and illustrations

The Reading Key series has five levels.

○ Reading Key **Preschool 1-6**
A six-book series designed for preschoolers and kindergarteners

Table of Contents | Preschool 1
Verbs

Unit **1** I Am, I Have · · · · · · · · · · 4

Unit **2** He Is, He Has · · · · · · · · · 12

Unit **3** I Am Running · · · · · · · · 20

Unit **4** You Are Sleeping · · · · · · · · 28

Review Test 1 · · · · · · · · · · · · · · · 36

Unit **5** I Run · · · · · · · · · · · · · · 38

Unit **6** She Runs · · · · · · · · · · · 46

Unit **7** Go, Went · · · · · · · · · · 54

Unit **8** Will, Be Going to · · · · · · · · 64

Review Test 2 · · · · · · · · · · · · · · 72

Word List · · · · · · · · · · · · · 74

Components Workbook for Daily Review • Answers and Translations

Syllabus | Preschool 1
Verbs

Subject	Unit	Grammar	Vocabulary
Be Verbs & Have, Has	Unit 1 **I Am, I Have**	Present simple: am, have	• I, am, have • Animals' names and features
	Unit 2 **He Is, He Has**	Present simple: is, has	• he, she, it, boy, girl, is, has • Animals' names and features
	Unit 3 **I Am Running**	Present continuous: be + V-ing	• walking, running, flying, swimming • singing, dancing • cooking, eating • I see
	Unit 4 **You Are Sleeping**	Present continuous: be + V-ing	• I, you, we, they, are • drinking, eating • sleeping, jumping
Common Verbs	Unit 5 **I Run**	Present simple: I/You/They/We run	• run, walk, swim, jump • well, fast, slowly • I like to
	Unit 6 **She Runs**	Present simple: He/She/It runs	• runs, sings, dances, swims, eats • She likes to
	Unit 7 **Go, Went**	Past simple: Regular and irregular verbs	• today, yesterday • eat/ate, go/went, do/did, come/came, see/saw, play/played
	Unit 8 **Will, Be Going to**	Future tense: will, be going to	• today, tomorrow • play soccer, play baseball, play a game, play with friends, ride a bike, watch TV, have a party

I Am, I Have

🎧 Key Words ➤ Read the words.

mane

trunk

lion

elephant

neck

mouth

giraffe

hippo

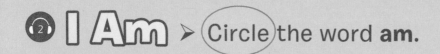

2 I Am ➤ (Circle) the word **am.**

I am Jane.
Who are you?

I (am) a lion.

I am a giraffe.

I am a hippo.

I am an elephant.

3 I Have ➤ Circle the word **have.**

I (have) two hands.

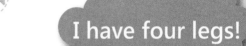

I have four legs!

I have two eyes.

I have two ears.

I have two legs.

Am or Have?

➤ Circle the correct word for each sentence.

I am a lion.
I (**am**, **have**) a mane.

I am a giraffe.
I (**am**, **have**) a long neck.

I am an elephant.
I (**am**, **have**) a trunk.

I am a hippo.
I (**am**, **have**) a big mouth.

⑤ Who Am I?

➤ <u>Draw lines</u> to match the sentences with each animal.

I have four legs.
I have a long **neck**.

elephant

I have four legs.
I have a **trunk**.

lion

I have four legs.
I have a **mane**.

giraffe

I have four legs.
I have a big **mouth**.

hippo

I Can Read

➤ Read the story. (Circle) the correct word for each sentence.

Animals in Africa

I am an elephant.
I have a (**trunk**, **mane**).

I am a lion.
I have a (**mane, trunk**).

I am a hippo.
I have a big (**mouth, mane**).

I am a giraffe.
I have a long (**neck, trunk**).

He Is, He Has

⑦ Key Words ➤ Read the words.

boy = he

girl = she

bird

rabbit

it

dog

cat

He Is, She Is, It Is

➤ Circle the word **is**.

The boy (is) Tom.

He **is** John.

The girl **is** Jane.

She **is** Julie.

It **is** a bird.

He Has, She Has, It Has

> ⊙(9) ➤ Circle the word **has.**

The girl (has) a cat.
She has a cat.

The boy has a dog.
He has a dog.

The girl has a rabbit.
She has a rabbit.

The boy has a bird.
He has a bird.

The bird has two wings.
It has two wings.

🎧 Have or Has?

➤ Circle the correct word for each sentence.

Jane

Tom

Julie

John

Who has the cat?
Jane (**have, has**) the cat.

Who has the dog?
Tom (**have, has**) the dog.

Who has the rabbit?
Julie (**have, has**) the rabbit.

Who has the bird?
John (**have, has**) the bird.

(11) What Is It?

➢ <u>Draw a line</u> to match the sentence with each animal.

▼ It has big eyes.

It is a hippo.

▼ It has a big mouth.

It is a cat.

▼ It has two wings.

It is a rabbit.

▼ It has long ears.

It is a bird.

I Can Read

➢ Read the story. Circle the correct word for each sentence.

Animal Friends

(She, He) is Jane.
She has a cat.
It has big eyes.

(She, He) is Jake.
He has a dog.
It has big ears.

She is Anna.
She (**has, have**) a bird.
It has two wings.

He is Tom.
He has a rabbit.
It (**has, have**) long ears.

I Am Running

Key Words ➤ Read the words.

walk

run

sing

swim

fly

cook

dance

eat

🔘 I Am Doing

➤ Circle the word with **-ing**.

I am flying.

I am running.

I am walking.

I am swimming.

🅙 What Are You Doing?

➤ Circle the correct word for each sentence.

I am a bird.
I am (**swimming**, **flying**).

I am a cat.
I am (**walking**, **running**).

I am a dog.
I am (**walking**, **running**).

I am a fish.
I am (**swimming**, **flying**).

I See

> Fill in the blanks with the words from the box.

walking	running	swimming	flying

I see a lion.
The lion is __walking__ .

I see a zebra.
The zebra is _____ .

I see a hippo.
The hippo is _____ .

I see a bird.
The bird is _____ .

17 Singing or Sing?

➤ Circle the correct word for each sentence.

I see a girl.
The girl is (singing, sing).

I see a boy.
The boy is (dancing, dance).

I see Mom.
Mom is (cook, cooking).

I see Tom.
He is (eat, eating).

I Can Read

> Read the story. (Circle) the correct word for each sentence.

What is Ann **doing**?
She is (**singing**, (**swimming**)).

What is Tom **doing**?
He is (**dancing**, **running**).

What is Mom **doing?**
She is (**flying, cooking**).

What is Ben **doing**?
He is (**eating, walking**).

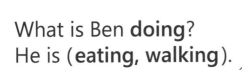

You Are Sleeping

⑲ Key Words ➤ Read the words.

I

you

we

he

she

they

eat

sleep

jump

You Are, They Are

➤ (Circle) the words **in blue.**

(I am) Ann.

You are **Tom.**

We are **friends.**

He is **a boy.**

They are **children.**

She is **a girl.**

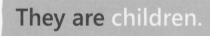

㉑ You Are Doing

➤ Circle the words with **-ing**.

I am eating.

You are drinking.

We are jumping.

They are sleeping.

What Are You Doing?

➤ Circle the correct word for each sentence.

I am Ann.
I am (**eating**, **drinking**) pizza.

You are Tom.
You are (**eating**, **drinking**) milk.

We are good friends.
We are (**jumping**, **sleeping**) together.

They are children.
They are (**jumping**, **sleeping**).

❶ What Are They Doing?

> ➤ Circle the correct word for each sentence.

I see lions.
They are (**sleeping** , **jumping**).

I see kangaroos.
They are (**sleeping** , **jumping**).

I see giraffes.
They are (**eating** , **drinking**) grass.

I see elephants.
They are (**eating** , **drinking**) water.

I Can Read

> Read the story. Circle the correct word for each sentence.

What are you **doing**?
I am (**eat,** **eating**) ice cream.

What are you **doing**?
I am (**drink, drinking**) milk.

What are they **doing**?
They are (**sleep, sleeping**).

What are they **doing**?
They are (**jump, jumping**) rope.

Review Test 1

A Choose and write.

| legs | eyes | ears | neck | mane | trunk |

1. eyes

2.

3.

4.

5.

6.

B Circle the correct word.

1.

I (**am**, **are**) Jane.

2.

You (**am**, **are**) Tom.

3.

She (**is**, **are**) a girl.

4.

He (**is**, **are**) a boy.

5.

It (**is**, **are**) a cat.

6.

They (**is**, **are**) children.

C Circle the correct word.

1.

   I am Julie.
   I (**have**, **has**) two hands.

2.

   You are a bird.
   You (**have**, **has**) two wings.

3.

   She is Ann.
   She (**have**, **has**) a dog.

4.

   It is an elephant.
   It (**have**, **has**) a trunk.

D Read and match.

1. I see lions.
   They are sleeping.

2. I see giraffes.
   They are eating grass.

3. I see a girl.
   She is eating a sandwich.

4. I see a boy.
   He is drinking water.

Unit 5 I Run

🎧25 Key Words

> Read the words and sentences.

rabbit

turtle

frog

dolphin

I run.

You walk.

We jump.

They swim.

Who Are You?

➤ (Circle) the words **in blue.**

I am a rabbit.

You are **a turtle.**

We are **frogs.**

They are **dolphins.**

🅰️ Run, Jump, Swim

➢ **Circle** the words **in blue**.

I am a rabbit.
I (run) fast.

You are a turtle.
You walk slowly.

We are frogs.
We jump well.

They are dolphins.
They swim well.

Sing, Dance

> Circle the correct word for each sentence.

I am a singer.
I (**sing**, **dance**) well.

You are a dancer.
You (**sing, dance**) well.

We are singers.
We (**sing, dance**) well.

They are dancers.
They (**sing, dance**) well.

29 I Like to

> Draw a line to match each picture and the sentence.

I like to sing.

 I am a singer.

I like to dance.

I am a dancer.

I like to swim.

I am a frog.

I like to jump.

I am a dolphin.

I Can Read

➤ Read the story. Circle the correct word for each sentence.

Who Am I?

- I like to dance.
- I dance well.
- I am a (dancer, singer).

I like to sing.
I sing well.
I am a (singer, dancer).

I like to run.
I (**run, swim**) fast.
I am a horse.

I like to swim.
I (**swim, run**) well.
I am a fish.

Unit 6 She Runs

Key Words

➤ Read the words and sentences.

she

he

it

She runs.

It runs.

He sings.

It sings.

32 I See ➤ (Circle) the words **in blue.**

I see a girl.
She (sings) well.

I see a boy.
He **dances** well.

I see a dolphin.
It **swims** fast.

I see a horse.
It **runs** fast.

³³ Sings, Dances

➤ Circle the correct word for each sentence.

The girl sings.
She (**sing**, **sings**) well.

The boy dances.
He (**dance**, **dances**) well.

The horse runs.
It (**run**, **runs**) fast.

The dolphin swims.
It (**swim**, **swims**) fast.

🎧34 She Likes to

> Draw a line to match the sentence with each picture.

She likes to walk. •

She likes to walk. • → •

He likes to run. •

She likes to swim. •

He likes to sleep. •

It likes to jump. •

Who Are They?

➤ Circle the correct word for each sentence.

She is Jane.
She (**like**, **likes**) to walk.

He is Tom.
He (**like**, **likes**) to run.

The girl is Ann.
She (**like**, **likes**) to swim.

It is a cat.
It (**like**, **likes**) to sleep.

It is a frog.
It (**like**, **likes**) to jump.

I Can Read

➤ Read the story. Circle the correct word for each sentence.

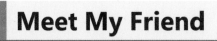

Meet My Friend

I have a dog.
His name is Sam.

He likes to run.
He (**run, runs**) fast.

He likes to jump.
He (**jump, jumps**) well.

He likes to dance.
He (**dance, dances**) well.

He likes to eat.
He (**eat, eats**) well.
He is fun.

Unit 7 Go, Went

Key Words ➤ Read the words.

school

park

movie

party

come home

do homework

play baseball

🎧 Eat, Ate

➤ (Circle) the word **eat**. Underline the word **ate**.

Today	Yesterday

I eat an apple.	I ate an apple.

I eat a banana.	I ate a banana.

I eat a sandwich.	I ate a sandwich.

I eat a cookie.	I ate a cookie.

Eat or Ate?

➤ (Circle) the correct word for each sentence.

Today, I eat an apple.

Yesterday, I (**eat**, **ate**) an apple, too.

Today, I eat a banana.

Yesterday, I (**eat**, **ate**) a banana, too.

Today, I eat a sandwich.

Yesterday, I (**eat**, **ate**) a sandwich, too.

Today, I eat a cookie.

Yesterday, I (**eat**, **ate**) a cookie, too.

Go, Went

40

> (Circle) the word **go**. Underline the word **went**.

Today		Yesterday

I (go) to school.

I <u>went</u> to school.

I go to the park.

I went to the park.

I go to a movie.

I went to a movie.

I go to a party.

I went to a party.

Go or Went?

➤ Circle the correct word for each sentence.

Today, I go to school.

Yesterday, I (**go,** **went**) to school, too.

Today, I go to the park.

Yesterday, I (**go,** **went**) to the park, too.

Today, I go to a movie.

Yesterday, I (**go,** **went**) to a movie, too.

Today, I go to a party.

Yesterday, I (**go,** **went**) to a party, too.

Do, Did

> (Circle) the words **in blue**. Underline the words **in re**

Today		Yesterday

I (do) my homework.

I <u>did</u> my homework.

I **come** home early.

I came home early.

I see a bird.

I saw a bird.

I **play** baseball.

I **played** baseball.

⁴³ Do or Did?

➤ Circle the correct word for each sentence.

Today, I do my homework.
Yesterday, I (**do, did**) my homework, too.

Today, I come home early.
Yesterday, I (**come, came**) home early, too.

Today, I see a bird.
Yesterday, I (**see, saw**) a bird, too.

Today, I play baseball.
Yesterday, I (**play, played**) baseball, too.

I Can Read

➤ Read the story. Circle the words **in blue.**

Yesterday, I was busy.

I went to school.

I went to the park.

I played baseball.

I went to a party.

I ate cake.
I ate pizza.
I ate ice cream.
I ate a cookie, too.

Unit 8 Will, Be Going to

🔊45 Key Words ➤ Read the words.

play soccer

play baseball

play a game

play with friends

ride a bike

watch TV

have a party

46 **I Will** ➤ (Circle) the word **will**.

Today		Tomorrow
I play soccer.		I (will) play soccer.
I play baseball.		I will play baseball.
I ride a bike.		I will ride a bike.
I watch TV.		I will watch TV.

What Will You Do?

➤ Circle the word **will**.

Today, I play soccer.
Tomorrow, I will play soccer, too.

Today, you play baseball.
Tomorrow, you will play baseball, too.

Today, we ride a bike.
Tomorrow, we will ride a bike, too.

Today, they watch TV.
Tomorrow, they will watch TV, too.

I Am Going to

> (Circle) the words **am going to** and **are going to**.

Today		Tomorrow
I go to school.		I (am going to) school.
I go to the park.		I am going to the park.
You play a game.		You are going to play a game.
You play with your friends.		You are going to play with your friends.

What Are You Going to Do?

➤ (Circle) the correct word for each sentence.

Today, I go to school.
Tomorrow, I (**am**, **are**) going to
school, too.

Today, I ride a bike.
Tomorrow, I am (**go**, **going**) to
ride a bike, too.

Today, you play a game.
Tomorrow, you are (**go**, **going**) to
play a game, too.

Today, you play with your friends.
Tomorrow, you are going to
(**play**, **played**) with your friends, too.

I Can Read

➤ Read the story. Circle the words
will and **are going to**.

My Birthday Party

Tomorrow is my birthday.
I will have a party.

My friends will come to my party.
Jane will come to my party.
Tina will come to my party.
Ben will come to my party, too.

We are going to eat cake.
We are going to eat pizza.
We are going to eat ice cream.
We are going to play a game, too.

The party will be fun.

Review Test 2

A Choose and write.

jump	run	swim	walk	dance	sing

1. run

2.

3.

4.

5.

6.

B Circle the correct word.

1.

I (**run**, **runs**) fast.

2.

You (**walk**, **walks**) slowly.

3.

We (**sing**, **sings**) well.

4.

They (**dance**, **dances**) well.

5.

He (**jump**, **jumps**) well.

6.

It (**swim**, **swims**) fast.

C Circle the correct word.

1.

   I (**like**, **likes**) to dance.
   I am a dancer.

2.

   You (**like**, **likes**) to sing.
   You are a singer.

3.

   He (**like**, **likes**) to run.
   He runs fast.

4.

   It (**like**, **likes**) to swim.
   It swims well.

D Choose and match.

1. Today, I come home early.
   Yesterday, I (**come**, **came**)
   home early, too.

2. Today, I see a bird.
   Yesterday, I (**see**, **saw**)
   a bird, too.

3. Today, I play soccer.
   Tomorrow, I will
   (**play**, **played**) soccer, too.

4. Today, I eat cake.
   Tomorrow, I am going to
   (**eat**, **ate**) cake, too.

Word List

Unit 1

I Am, I Have
我是，我有

1. **lion** 狮子
2. **mane** 鬃毛
3. **elephant** 大象
4. **trunk** 象鼻
5. **giraffe** 长颈鹿
6. **neck** 脖子
7. **long neck** 长脖子
8. **hippo** 河马
9. **mouth** 嘴巴
10. **big mouth** 大嘴巴
11. **I am** 我是
12. **I have** 我有
13. **who** 谁
14. **Who are you?** 你是谁?
15. **hand** 手 *two hands 两只手
16. **leg** 脚 *two legs 两只脚
17. **eye** 眼睛 *two eyes 两只眼睛
18. **ear** 耳朵 *two ears 两只耳朵
19. **Who am I?** 我是谁?
20. **animal** 动物 *复数: animals 动物们
21. **in Africa** 在非洲

Unit 2

He Is, He Has
他是，他有

1. **boy** 男孩
2. **he** 他
3. **girl** 女孩
4. **she** 她
5. **cat** 猫
6. **dog** 狗
7. **rabbit** 兔子
8. **bird** 鸟
9. **it** 它
10. **He is** 他是……
11. **She is** 她是……
12. **It is** 它是……

13	**He has**	他有	
14	**She has**	她有	
15	**It has**	它有	
16	**wing**	翅膀 *two wings 两只翅膀	

13 **He has** 他有
14 **She has** 她有
15 **It has** 它有
16 **wing** 翅膀 *two wings 两只翅膀

Unit 3

I Am Running
我正在跑步

1 **walk** 走路
2 **run** 跑步
3 **fly** 飞
4 **swim** 游泳
5 **sing** 唱歌
6 **dance** 跳舞
7 **cook** 烹饪
8 **eat** 吃
9 **doing** 正在做……
10 **I am doing** 我正在做……
11 **walking** 正在走路
12 **running** 正在跑步
13 **flying** 正在飞
14 **swimming** 正在游泳
15 **what** 什么（疑问代词）
16 **What are you doing?** 你正在做什么?
17 **fish** 鱼
18 **see** 看见

19 **zebra** 斑马
20 **Mom** 妈妈
21 **What is Ann doing?** 安正在做什么?

Unit 4

You Are Sleeping
你正在睡觉

1 **I** 我
2 **you** 你
3 **we** 我们
4 **he** 他
5 **she** 她
6 **they** 他们
7 **eat** 吃
8 **drink** 喝
9 **sleep** 睡
10 **jump** 跳
11 **You are** 你是……
12 **They are** 他们是……
13 **We are** 我们是……
14 **friend** 朋友 *复数: friends 朋友们
15 **children** 孩子们
16 **eating** 正在吃
17 **drinking** 正在喝
18 **jumping** 正在跳
19 **sleeping** 正在睡
20 **drink milk** 喝牛奶

21	**together**	一起
22	**eat grass**	吃草
23	**drink water**	喝水
24	**jump rope**	跳绳

Unit 5

I Run 我跑

1	**rabbit**	兔子
2	**turtle**	乌龟
3	**frog**	青蛙
4	**dolphin**	海豚
5	**run**	跑
6	**walk**	走
7	**jump**	跳
8	**swim**	游泳
9	**Who are you?**	你是谁？
10	**fast**	快速的，迅速的
11	**slowly**	缓慢地
12	**well**	很好地
13	**sing**	唱歌
14	**dance**	跳舞
15	**singer**	歌手 *复数: singers 歌手们
16	**dancer**	舞者 *复数: dancers 舞者们
17	**like to**	喜欢（后接动词原形）
18	**horse**	马
19	**fish**	鱼

Unit 6

She Runs 她跑

1	**run**	跑
	*runs: run 的第三人称单数	
2	**sing**	唱
	*sings: sing 的第三人称单数	
3	**dance**	跳舞
	*dances: dance 的第三人称单数	
4	**swim**	游泳
	*swims: swim 的第三人称单数	
5	**like to**	喜欢
	*likes to: like to 的第三人称单数	
6	**meet**	认识
7	**my friend**	我的朋友
8	**name**	名字
9	**fun**	有趣的；愉快的

Unit 7

Go, Went
去（go 的现在式），
去（go 的过去式）

1	**school**	学校
2	**park**	公园
3	**movie**	电影
4	**party**	派对
5	**come home**	回家
6	**do homework**	做功课
7	**play baseball**	打棒球

8	eat	吃
9	ate	吃 *eat 的过去式
10	apple	苹果
11	banana	香蕉
12	sandwich	三明治
13	cookie	饼干
14	today	今天
15	yesterday	昨天
16	too	也
17	go	去
18	went	去 *go 的过去式
19	go to school	上学
20	go to the park	去公园
21	go to a movie	去看电影
22	go to a party	去派对
23	do	做
24	did	做 *do 的过去式
25	come	来
26	came	来 *come 的过去式
27	see	看见
28	saw	看见 *see 的过去式
29	play	玩
30	played	玩 *play 的过去式
31	busy	忙碌的

Unit 8

Will, Be Going to
将要，即将要去

1	play soccer	踢足球
2	play baseball	打棒球
3	play a game	玩游戏
4	play with friends	跟朋友一起玩
5	ride	骑
6	ride a bike	骑自行车
7	watch	观看；注视
8	watch TV	看电视
9	have a party	举办派对
10	will	将要
11	tomorrow	明天
12	be going to	即将要去……
13	birthday	生日
14	birthday party	生日派对

Workbook

Daily Test 1

I Am, I Have

A Read and write.

1.
lion
lion

2.
elephant
elephant

3.
giraffe
giraffe

4.
hippo
hippo

B Match and write.

- 1. trunk   trunk
- 2. mane   mane
- 3. neck   neck
- 4. mouth   mouth
- 5. hands   hands
- 6. legs   legs

C **Circle the correct word for each sentence.**

1.

I am a (**hippo** , **giraffe**).

2.

I am an (**elephant, lion**).

3.

I am a (**giraffe, lion**).

4.

I am a (**lion, elephant**).

D **Choose and write.**

hands	neck	ears	mane	trunk	mouth

1.

I have two ___**hands**___ .

2.

I have two _____.

3.

I have a _____.

4.

I have a long _____.

5.

I have a big _____.

6.

I have a _____.

Daily Test 2

He Is, He Has

A Read and write.

1.

boy   he

boy   he

2.

girl   she

girl   she

3.

cat   dog   rabbit   bird

cat   dog   rabbit   bird

B Match and write.

1. it   it

2. she   she

3. he   he

4. wings   wings

5. ears   ears

6. eyes   eyes

C Circle the correct word for each sentence.

1.

The boy (**is, has**) Tom.

2.

He (**is, has**) John.

3.

The girl (**is, has**) Jane.

4.

She (**is, has**) Julie.

D Choose and write.

| eyes | ears | mouth | wings |

1.

It has big __eyes__ .

2.

It has a big _____ .

3.

It has two _____ .

4.

It has long _____ .

Daily Test 3

I Am Running

A Read and write.

1.

walk   run

walk   run

2.

fly   swim

fly   swim

3.

sing   dance

sing   dance

4.

cook   eat

cook   eat

B Match and write.

1. walking   walking   

2. running   running

3. flying   flying

4. swimming   swimming

5. singing   singing

6. dancing   dancing   

C Circle the correct word for each sentence.

1.
I am (**walking**, **running**).

2.
I am (**walking**, **running**).

3.
I am (**swimming**, **flying**).

4.
I am (**swimming**, **flying**).

D Choose and write.

eating   dancing   cooking   singing

1.
The girl is ___**singing**___.

2.
The boy is _____.

3.
Mom is _____.

4.
Tom is _____.

Daily Test 4

You Are Sleeping

A Read and write.

1.

I   you   we

I   you   we

2.

he   she   they

he   she   they

B Match and write.

1. friends   friends   •

2. children   children   •

3. eat   eat   •

4. drink   drink   •

5. sleep   sleep   •

6. jump   jump   •

86

C. Circle the correct word for each sentence.

1.

I (**am**, **are**) Ann.

2.

You (**am**, **are**) Tom.

3.

We (**is**, **are**) friends.

4.

They (**is**, **are**) children.

5.

He (**is**, **are**) a boy.

6.

She (**is**, **are**) a girl.

D. Choose and write.

| jumping | eating | drinking | sleeping |

1.

I am __eating__ pizza.

2.

You are _____ milk.

3.

We are _____ together.

4.

They are _____.

Daily Test 5

I Run

A Read and write.

1.

rabbit

rabbit

2.

turtle

turtle

3.

frog

frog

4.

dolphin

dolphin

B Match and write.

- 1. I run.

I run.

- 2. You walk.

You walk.

- 3. We jump.

We jump.

- 4. They swim.

They swim.

C Circle the correct word for each sentence.

1.

I am a rabbit.
I (**run**, **swim**) fast.

2.

You are a turtle.
You (**walk, sing**) slowly.

3.

We are frogs.
We (**jump, sing**) well.

4.

They are dolphins.
They (**swim, run**) well.

D Choose and write.

sing	run	like	swim

1.

I __**like**__ to dance.
I dance well.

2.

I like to sing.
I _____ well.

3.

I like to run.
I _____ fast.

4.

I like to swim.
I _____ well.

Daily Test 6

She Runs

A Read and write.

1.

she

he

it

she   he   it

2.

She runs.

It sings.

She runs.   It sings.

B Match and write.

1. She sings well.

   She sings well.

2. He dances well.

   He dances well.

3. It swims fast.

   It swims fast.

4. It runs fast.

   It runs fast.

C Circle the correct word for each sentence.

1.

   I see a girl.
   She (**sing,** (**sings**)) well.

2.

   I see a boy.
   He (**dance, dances**) well.

3.

   I see a fish.
   It (**swim, swims**) fast.

4.

   I see a horse.
   It (**run, runs**) fast.

D Choose and write.

| likes | eats | jumps | dances |

1. He ___**likes**___ to run.
   He runs fast.

2. He likes to jump.
   He _____ well.

3. He likes to dance.
   He _____ well.

4. He likes to eat.
   He _____ well.

Daily Test 7

Go, Went

A Read and write.

1.
school

school

2.
park

park

3.
movie

movie

4.
party

party

B Match and write.

1. come home   come home •

2. go to school   go to school •

3. do homework   do homework •

4. play baseball   play baseball •

5. see a bird   see a bird •

6. eat an apple   eat an apple •

C Circle the correct word for each sentence.

1.
Yesterday, I (**go**, (**went**)) to school.

2.
Yesterday, I (**come, came**) home early.

3.
Yesterday, I (**eat, ate**) an apple.

4.
Yesterday, I (**do, did**) my homework.

5.
Yesterday, I (**see, saw**) a bird.

6.
Yesterday, I (**play, played**) baseball.

D Choose and write.

| went to | saw | played | ate |

1.
Yesterday, I __saw__ a bird.
I _____ baseball.

2.
Yesterday, I _____ a party.
I _____ cake.

Daily Test

8 Will, Be Going to

A Read and write.

1.
soccer
soccer

2.
baseball
baseball

3.
bike
bike

4.
birthday
birthday

B Match and write.

- 1. play soccer _play soccer_
- 2. play a game _play a game_
- 3. play with friends _play with friends_
- 4. ride a bike _ride a bike_
- 5. watch TV _watch TV_
- 6. have a party _have a party_

C Circle the correct word for each sentence.

1. Tomorrow, I will ((**play**, **played**) soccer.

2. Tomorrow, you will (**go, went**) to school.

3. Tomorrow, I am (**go, going**) to the park.

4. Tomorrow, you are going to (**play, played**) a game.

D Choose and write.

| eat | have | come | going to | play |

1. Tomorrow, I will ___**have**___ a party.

2. My friends will _____ to my party.

3. We are _____ eat cake.

4. We are going to _____ pizza.

5. We are going to _____ a game.

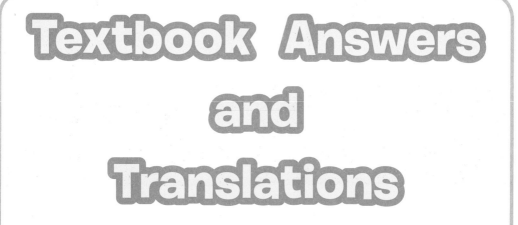

Textbook Answers and Translations

课本解答与翻译

⑧ Am or Have? "是" 或 "有"?
圈出每个句子中正确的单词。

I am a lion.
I (**am**, (**have**)) a mane.

我是一只狮子。
我（是；有）鬃毛。

I am a giraffe.
I (**am**, (**have**)) a long neck.

我是一只长颈鹿。
我（是；有）长脖子。

I am an elephant.
I (**am**, (**have**)) a trunk.

我是一只大象。
我（是；有）象鼻。

I am a hippo.
I (**am**, (**have**)) a big mouth.

我是一头河马。
我（是；有）大嘴巴。

⑨ Who Am I? 我是谁?
将每组句子连接到正确的动物。

I have four legs.
I have a long neck.

我有四条腿。
我有长脖子。

elephant 大象

I have four legs.
I have a trunk.

我有四条腿。
我有象鼻。

lion 狮子

I have four legs.
I have a mane.

我有四条腿。
我有鬃毛。

giraffe 长颈鹿

I have four legs.
I have a big mouth.

我有四条腿。
我有大嘴巴。

hippo 河马

⑩ I Can Read 我会阅读
阅读故事，并圈出每个句子中正确的单词。

Animals in Africa 非洲的动物

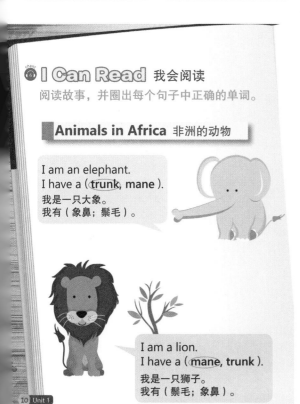

I am an elephant.
I have a ((**trunk**), mane).

我是一只大象。
我有（象鼻；鬃毛）。

I am a lion.
I have a ((**mane**), trunk).

我是一只狮子。
我有（鬃毛；象鼻）。

I am a hippo.
I have a big ((**mouth**), mane).

我是一只河马。
我有大（嘴巴；鬃毛）。

I am a giraffe.
I have a long ((**neck**), trunk).

我是一只长颈鹿。
我有长（脖子；象鼻）。

Textbook Answers and Translations 99

Have or Has?

有（第一、二人称）；有（第三人称）

圈出每个句子中正确的单词。

Jane 简

Who has the cat? 猫是谁的？
Jane (**have**, (**has**)) the cat. 猫是简的。

Who has the dog? 狗是谁的？
Tom (**have**, (**has**)) the dog. 狗是汤姆的。

Who has the rabbit? 兔子是谁的？
Julie (**have**, (**has**)) the rabbit. 兔子是茱莉的。

Who has the bird? 鸟是谁的？
John (**have**, (**has**)) the bird. 鸟是约翰的。

Tom 汤姆

Julie 茱莉

John 约翰

What Is It? 它是什么？

将每个句子连接到正确的动物。

▼ It has big eyes.
它有大眼睛。

It is a hippo.
它是一只河马。

▼ It has a big mouth.
它有大嘴巴。

It is a cat.
它是一只猫。

▼ It has two wings.
它有一对翅膀。

It is a rabbit.
它是一只兔子。

▼ It has long ears.
它有长耳朵。

It is a bird.
它是一只鸟。

⑯ I See 我看见……

在空格中填入正确的单词。

walking   running   swimming   flying

I see a lion.
The lion is __walking__ .

我看到一只狮子。
那只狮子正在走路。

I see a zebra.
The zebra is __running__ .

我看到一只斑马。
那只斑马正在跑步。

I see a hippo.
The hippo is __swimming__ .

我看到一只河马。
那只河马正在游泳。

I see a bird.
The bird is __flying__ .

我看到一只鸟。
那只鸟正在飞。

⑰ Singing or Sing? 正在唱歌还是唱歌?

圈出句子中正确的单词。

I see a girl.
The girl is (singing, sing).

我看到一个女孩。
女孩(正在唱歌;唱歌)。

I see a boy.
The boy is (dancing, dance).

我看到一个男孩。
男孩(正在跳舞;跳舞)。

I see Mom.
Mom is (cook, cooking).

我看到妈妈。
妈妈(煮饭;正在煮饭)。

I see Tom.
He is (eat, eating).

我看到汤姆。
汤姆(吃东西;正在吃东西)。

⑱ I Can Read 我会阅读

阅读故事,并圈出每个句子中正确的单词。

What is Ann doing?
She is (singing, swimming).

安正在做什么?
她(正在唱歌;正在游泳)。

What is Tom doing?
He is (dancing, running).

汤姆正在做什么?
他(正在跳舞;正在跑步)。

What is Mom doing?
She is (flying, cooking).

妈妈正在做什么?
她(正在飞;正在煮饭)。

What is Ben doing?
He is (eating, walking).

本正在做什么?
他(正在吃东西;正在走路)。

Textbook Answers and Translations 103

Unit 4 You Are Sleeping
你正在睡觉

Key Words 关键词汇
阅读以下单词。

I 我
you 你
we 我们
he 他
she 她
they 他们

eat 吃
drink 喝
sleep 睡觉
jump 跳

You Are, They Are 你是；他们是……
圈出蓝色的单词。

I am Ann. 我是安。
You are Tom. 你是汤姆。
We are friends. 我们是朋友。
He is a boy. 他是男孩。
They are children. 他们是朋友。
She is a girl. 她是女孩。

You Are Doing 你正在……
圈出含有-ing的单词。

I am eating. 我正在吃。
You are drinking. 你正在喝。
We are jumping. 我们正在跳。
They are sleeping. 他们正在睡觉。

28 Unit 4

Unit 4 29

30 Unit 4

Unit 4 31

104 Textbook Answers and Translations

What Are You Doing?
你们正在做什么?
圈出句子中正确的单词。

I am Ann.
I am (**eating**, drinking) pizza.
我是安。
我（正在吃；正在喝）比萨。

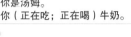

You are Tom.
You are (eating, **drinking**) milk.
你是汤姆。
你（正在吃；正在喝）牛奶。

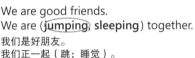

We are good friends.
We are (**jumping**, sleeping) together.
我们是好朋友。
我们正一起（跳；睡觉）。

They are children.
They are (jumping, **sleeping**).
他们是小孩。
他们一起正（跳；睡觉）。

What Are They Doing?
它们正在做什么?
圈出句子中正确的单词。

I see lions.
They are (**sleeping**, jumping).
我看见狮子。
它们（正在睡觉；正在跳）。

I see kangaroos.
They are (sleeping, **jumping**).
我看见袋鼠。
它们（正在睡觉；正在跳）。

I see giraffes.
They are (**eating**, drinking) grass.
我看见长颈鹿。
它们（正在吃；正在喝）草。

I see elephants.
They are (eating, **drinking**) water.
我看见大象。
它们（正在吃；正在喝）水。

I Can Read 我会阅读
阅读故事，并圈出每个句子中正确的单词。

What are you **doing**?
I am (eat, **eating**) ice cream.
你正在做什么?
我（吃；正在吃）冰淇淋。

What are you **doing**?
I am (drink, **drinking**) milk.
你正在做什么?
我（喝；正在喝）牛奶。

What are they **doing**?
They are (sleep, **sleeping**).
他们正在做什么?
他们（睡觉；正在睡觉）。

What are they **doing**?
They are (jump, **jumping**) rope.
他们正在做什么?
他们（跳；正在跳）绳。

Review Test 1

A **Choose and write.** 选出正确的字词并填入空格。

| legs | eyes | ears | neck | mane | trunk |

1. eyes 眼睛
2. neck 脖子
3. legs 腿
6. trunk 象鼻
4. ears 耳朵
5. mane 鬃毛

B Circle the correct word. 圈出正确的单词。

1.

I (**am**, are) Jane.
我（是；是）简。

2.

You (**am**, **are**) Tom.
你（是；是）汤姆。

3.

She (**is**, are) a girl.
她（是；是）一个女孩。

4.

He (**is**, are) a boy.
他（是；是）一位男孩。

5.

It (**is**, are) a cat.
它是一只猫。

6.

They (is, **are**) children.
他们是小孩。

36 Review Test

Circle the correct word.　圈出正确的单词。

1.

I am Julie.
I (**have**, **has**) two hands.
我是茉莉。
我（有；有）两只手。

2.

You are a bird.
You (**have**, **has**) two wings.
你是一只小鸟。
你（有；有）两只翅膀。

3.

She is Ann.
She (**have**, **has**) a dog.
她是安。
她（有；有）一只狗。

4.

It is an elephant.
It (**have**, **has**) a trunk.
它是一只大象。
它（有；有）一个象鼻。

Review Test　37

D **Read and match.** 阅读句子，并连接到正确的图片。

1.
I see lions.
They are sleeping.
我看到狮子。
它们正在睡觉。

2.
I see giraffes.
They are eating grass.
我看到长颈鹿。
它们正在吃草。

3.
I see a girl.
She is eating a sandwich.
我看到一个女孩。
她正在吃三明治。

4.
I see a boy.
He is drinking water.
我看到一个男孩。
他正在喝水。

Review Test 37

Unit 5 I Run 我跑

Key Words 关键词汇

阅读下面的单词与句子。

frog
青蛙

turtle
乌龟

rabbit
兔子

dolphin
海豚

I run.
我跑。

We jump.
我们跳。

They swim.
它们游泳。

You walk.
你走。

38 Unit 5

Who Are You? 你是谁？
圈出蓝色的单词。

You are a turtle.
你是一只乌龟。

I am a rabbit.
我是一只兔子。

We are frogs.
我们是青蛙。

They are dolphins.
它们是海豚。

Run, Jump, Swim
跑步；跳；游泳
圈出蓝色的单词。

I am a rabbit. 我是一只兔子。
I run fast. 我跑得很快。

You are a turtle. 你是一只乌龟。
You walk slowly. 你走得很慢。

We are frogs. 我们是青蛙。
We jump well. 我们很会跳。

They are dolphins. 他们是海豚。
They swim well. 他们很会游泳。

Sing, Dance 唱歌；跳舞
圈出句子中正确的单词。

I am a singer. 我是一位歌手。
I (sing, dance) well. 我（唱得；跳得）很好。

You are a dancer. 你是一名舞者。
You (sing, dance) well. 你（唱得；跳得）很好。

We are singers. 我们是歌手。
We (sing, dance) well. 我们（唱得；跳得）很好。

他们是舞者。
They are dancers. 他们（唱得；跳得）很好。
They (sing, dance) well.

I Like to 我喜欢……
将图片连接到描述正确的句子。

I like to sing.
我喜欢唱歌。

I like to dance.
我喜欢跳舞。

I like to swim.
我喜欢游泳。

I like to jump.
我喜欢跳。

I am a singer.
我是一位歌手。

I am a dancer.
我是一位舞者。

I am a frog.
我是一只青蛙。

I am a dolphin.
我是一只海豚。

I Can Read 我会阅读

阅读故事，并圈出句子中正确的单词。

Who Am I? 我是谁?

I like to dance.
I dance well.
I am a (dancer, singer).

我喜欢跳舞。
我跳得很好。
我是一位（舞者；歌手）。

I like to sing.
I sing well.
I am a (singer, dancer).

我喜欢唱歌。
我唱得很好。
我是一位（歌手；舞者）。

I like to run.
I (run, swim) fast.
I am a horse.

我喜欢跑步。
我（跑得；游得）很快。
我是一只马。

I like to swim.
I (swim, run) well.
I am a fish.

我喜欢游泳。
我很会（游泳；跑）。
我是一条鱼。

Unit 6 She Runs
她跑

Key Words 关键词汇

阅读下面的单词与句子。

she
她

he
他

it
它

She runs.
她跑。

It runs.
它跑。

He sings.
他唱。

It sings.
它唱。

◉ I See 我看到……

圈出蓝色的单词。

I see a girl.
She (sings) well.
我看见一个女孩。
她唱得很好。

I see a boy.
He (dances) well.
我看见一个男孩。
他舞跳得很好。

I see a dolphin.
It (swims) fast.
我看见一只海豚。
它游得很快。

I see a horse.
It (runs) fast.
我看见一只马。
它跑得很快。

◉ Sings, Dances 唱歌；跳舞

圈出句子中正确的单词。

The girl sings.
She (sing, **sings**) well.
女孩在唱歌。
她（唱得；唱得）很好。

The boy dances.
He (dance, **dances**) well.
男孩在跳舞。
他（跳得；跳得）很好。

The horse runs.
It (run, **runs**) fast.
马在奔跑。
它（跑得；跑得）很快。

The dolphin swims.
It (swim, **swims**) fast.
海豚在游泳。
它（游得；游得）很快。

◉ She Likes to 她喜欢……

将句子连接到描述正确的图片。

She likes to walk.
她喜欢走路。

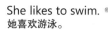

He likes to run.
他喜欢跑步。

She likes to swim.
她喜欢游泳。

He likes to sleep.
他喜欢睡觉。

It likes to jump.
它喜欢跳。

◉ Who Are They? 他们是谁?

圈出句子中正确的单词。

She is Jane.
She (like, **likes**) to walk.
她是简。
她喜欢走路。

He is Tom.
He (like, **likes**) to run.
他是汤姆。
他喜欢跑步。

The girl is Ann.
She (like, **likes**) to swim.
这个女孩是珍。
她喜欢游泳。

It is a cat.
It (like, **likes**) to sleep.
它是一只猫。
它喜欢睡觉。

It is a frog.
It (like, **likes**) to jump.
它是一只青蛙。
它喜欢跳。

Textbook Answers and Translations 113

Eat, Ate

eat（吃）的现在式；eat（吃）的过去式

圈出单词eat，在单词ate下面画线。

Today 今天	Yesterday 昨天
I **eat** an apple. 我吃一个苹果。	I <u>ate</u> an apple. 我吃了一个苹果。
I **eat** a banana. 我吃一根香蕉。	I <u>ate</u> a banana. 我吃了一根香蕉。
I **eat** a sandwich. 我吃一个三明治。	I <u>ate</u> a sandwich. 我吃了一个三明治。
I **eat** a cookie. 我吃一块饼干。	I <u>ate</u> a cookie. 我吃了一块饼干。

Eat or Ate?

eat 的现在式或过去式？

圈出句子中正确的单词。

Today, I eat an apple.
Yesterday, I (**eat**, (**ate**)) an apple, too.
今天，我吃一个苹果。
昨天，我也（吃；吃了）一个苹果。

Today, I eat a banana.
Yesterday, I (**eat**, (**ate**)) a banana, too.
今天，我吃一根香蕉。
昨天，我也（吃；吃了）一根香蕉。

Today, I eat a sandwich.
Yesterday, I (**eat**, (**ate**)) a sandwich, too.
今天，我吃一个三明治。
昨天，我也（吃；吃了）一个三明治。

Today, I eat a cookie.
Yesterday, I (**eat**, (**ate**)) a cookie, too.
今天，我吃一块饼干。
昨天，我也（吃；吃了）一块饼干。

Go, Went

go（去）的现在式；go（去）的过去式

圈出单词go，在单词went下面画线。

Today 今天	Yesterday 昨天
I **go** to school. 我去上学。	I <u>went</u> to school. 我去上了学。
I **go** to the park. 我去公园。	I <u>went</u> to the park. 我去了公园。
I **go** to a movie. 我去看电影。	I <u>went</u> to a movie. 我去看了电影。
I **go** to a party. 我去派对。	I <u>went</u> to a party. 我去了派对。

Go or Went?

go 的现在式或过去式？

圈出句子中正确的单词。

Today, I go to school.
Yesterday, I (**go**, (**went**)) to school, too.
今天，我也上学。
昨天，我也（去；去了）学校。

Today, I go to the park.
Yesterday, I (**go**, (**went**)) to the park, too.
今天，我去公园。
昨天，我也（去；去了）公园。

Today, I go to a movie.
Yesterday, I (**go**, (**went**)) to a movie, too.
今天，我去看电影。
昨天，我也去（看；看了）电影。

Today, I go to a party.
Yesterday, I (**go**, (**went**)) to a party, too.
今天，我去派对。
昨天，我也（去；去了）派对。

Do, Did
do（做）的现在式；do（做）的过去式
圈出蓝色的单词，在红色的单词下面画线。

Today 今天	Yesterday 昨天

I **do** my homework.
我做我的功课。

I did my homework.
我做了我的功课。

I **come** home early.
我很早回家。

I came home early.
我很早回了家。

I **see** a bird.
我看到一只鸟。

I saw a bird.
我看到了一只鸟。

I **play** baseball.
我打棒球。

I played baseball.
我打了棒球。

60 Unit 7

Do or Did?
do 的现在式或过去式？
圈出句子中正确的单词。

Today, I do my homework.
Yesterday, I (**do**, **did**) my homework, too.
今天，我做我的功课。
昨天，我也（做；做了）我的功课。

Today, I come home early.
Yesterday, I (**come**, **came**) home early, too.
今天，我很早回家。
昨天，我也很早（回；回了）家。

Today, I see a bird.
Yesterday, I (**see**, **saw**) a bird, too.
今天，我看到一只鸟。
昨天，我也（看到；看到了）一只鸟。

Today, I play baseball.
Yesterday, I (**play**, **played**) baseball, too.
今天，我打棒球。
昨天，我也（打；打了）棒球。

Unit 7 61

I Can Read 我会阅读
阅读故事，并圈出蓝色的单词。

Yesterday, I was busy. 昨天，我很忙。

I **went to** school.
我去了学校。

I **went to** a party.
我去了派对。

I **went to** the park.
我去了公园。

62 Unit 8

I **played** baseball.
我打了棒球。

I **ate** cake.
I **ate** pizza.
I **ate** ice cream.
I **ate** a cookie, too.
我吃了蛋糕。
我吃了比萨。
我吃了冰淇淋。
我也吃了饼干。

Unit 8 63

Unit 8 Will, Be Going to
将；即将要

Key Words 关键词汇
阅读下面的单词。

play soccer
踢足球

play baseball
打棒球

play a game
玩游戏

play with friends
和朋友玩

ride a bike
骑自行车

watch TV
看电视

have a party
举办派对

I Will 我将会……
圈出单词will。

Today 今天	Tomorrow 明天
I play soccer. 我踢足球。	I will play soccer. 我将会踢足球。
I play baseball. 我打棒球。	I will play baseball. 我将会打棒球。
I ride a bike. 我骑自行车。	I will ride a bike. 我将会骑自行车。
I watch TV. 我看电视。	I will watch TV. 我将会看电视。

What Will You Do?
你将会做什么？
圈出单词will。

Today, I play soccer.
Tomorrow, I will play soccer, too.
今天，我踢足球。
明天，我也会踢足球。

Today, you play baseball.
Tomorrow, you will play baseball, too.
今天，你打棒球。
明天，你也会打棒球。

Today, we ride a bike.
Tomorrow, we will ride a bike, too.
今天，我们骑自行车。
明天，我们也会骑自行车。

Today, they watch TV.
Tomorrow, they will watch TV, too.
今天，他们看电视。
明天，他们也会看电视。

I Am Going to 我将要……
圈出am going to和are going to。

Today 今天	Tomorrow 明天
I go to school. 我去上学。	I am going to go to school. 我将要去上学。
I go to the park. 我去公园。	I am going to go to the park. 我将要去公园。
You play a game. 你玩游戏。	You are going to play a game. 你将要去玩游戏。
You play with your friends. 你和朋友们一起玩。	You are going to play with your friends. 你将要和朋友们一起玩。

68 Unit 8

What Are You Going to Do?
你将要做什么？
圈出句子中正确的单词。

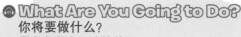

Today, I go to school.
Tomorrow, I (am, are) going to go to school, too.
今天，我去上学。
明天，我也要去上学。

Today, I ride a bike.
Tomorrow, I am (go, going) to ride a bike, too.
今天，我骑自行车。
明天，我也要骑自行车。

Today, you play a game.
Tomorrow, you are (go, going) to play a game, too.
今天，你玩游戏。
明天，你也要玩游戏。

Today, you play with your friends.
Tomorrow, you are going to
(play, played) with your friends, too.
今天，你和朋友们一起玩。
明天，你也要和朋友们一起玩。

Unit 8 69

I Can Read 我会阅读
圈出will和are going to。

My Birthday Party
我的生日派对

Tomorrow is my birthday.
I will have a party.
明天是我的生日。
我将举办一个派对。

My friends will come to my party.
Jane will come to my party.
Tina will come to my party.
Ben will come to my party, too.
我的朋友们会参加我的派对。
简会参加我的派对。
蒂娜会参加我的派对。
本也会参加我的派对。

70 Unit 8

We are going to eat cake.
We are going to eat pizza.
We are going to eat ice cream.
We are going to play a game, too.

我们将要吃蛋糕。
我们将要吃比萨。
我们将要吃冰淇淋。
我们也要玩游戏。

The party will be fun.
派对会很有趣。

Unit 8 71

118 Textbook Answers and Translations

Review Test 2

A Choose and write. 选出正确的单词并填入空格。

jump   run   swim   walk   dance   sing

1. run 跑

2. walk 走路

3. jump 跳

4. swim 游泳

5. sing 唱歌

6. dance 跳舞

B Circle the correct word. 圈出句子中正确的单词。

1. I (**run**, **runs**) fast.
    我（跑得；跑得）很快。

2. You (**walk**, **walks**) slowly.
    你（走得；走得）很慢。

3. We (**sing**, **sings**) well.
    我们（唱得；唱得）不错。

4. They (**dance**, **dances**) well.
    他们舞（跳得；跳得）不错。

5. He (**jump**, **jumps**) well.
    他（跳得；跳得）很好。

6. It (**swim**, **swims**) fast.
    它（游得；游得）很快。

ⓒ Circle the correct word. 圈出句子中正确的单词。

1.

I (**like**, **likes**) to dance.
I am a dancer.
我（喜欢；喜欢）跳舞。
我是一名舞者。

2.

You (**like**, **likes**) to sing.
You are a singer.
你（喜欢；喜欢）唱歌。
你是一位歌手。

3.

He (**like**, **likes**) to run.
He runs fast.
他（喜欢；喜欢）跑步。
他跑得很快。

4.

It (**like**, **likes**) to swim.
It swims well.
它（喜欢；喜欢）游泳。
它游得很好。

Review Test 73

D Choose and match. 圈出正确的单词，并连接到正确的图片。

1. Today, I come home early.
Yesterday, I (**come**, **came**)
home early, too.
今天，我很早回家。
昨天，我也很早（回；回了）家。

2. Today, I see a bird.
Yesterday, I (**see**, **saw**) a
bird, too.
今天，我看见一只小鸟。
昨天，我也（看见；看见了）
一只小鸟。

3. Today, I play soccer.
Tomorrow, I will (**play**,
played) soccer, too.
今天，我玩足球。
明天，我也会（玩；玩了）足球。

4. Today, I eat cake.
Tomorrow, I am going to (**eat**,
ate) cake, too.
今天，我吃蛋糕。
明天，我也会（吃；吃了）蛋糕。

Review Test 73

Daily Test Answers

单元练习解答

I Am, I Have

A Read and write.

1.

lion

lion

2.

elephant

elephant

3.

giraffe

giraffe

4.

hippo

hippo

80

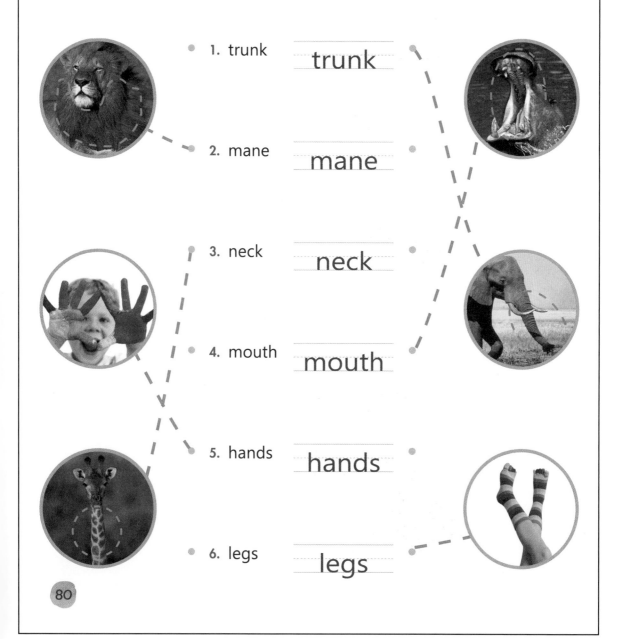

1. trunk   trunk

2. mane   mane

3. neck   neck

4. mouth   mouth

5. hands   hands

6. legs   legs

80

ⓒ **Circle the correct word for each sentence.**

1.

I am a (**hippo**, **giraffe**).

2.

I am an (**elephant**, **lion**).

3.

I am a (**giraffe**, **lion**).

4.

I am a (**lion**, **elephant**).

D **Choose and write.**

| hands | neck | ears | mane | trunk | mouth |

1.

I have two ___hands___ .

2.

I have two __ears__ .

3.

I have a __mane__ .

4.

I have a long __neck__ .

5.

I have a big __mouth__ .

6.

I have a __trunk__ .

81

A Read and write.

1.

boy   he

boy   he

2.

girl   she

girl   she

3.

cat

cat

dog

dog

rabbit

rabbit

bird

bird

82

B Match and write.

1. it

it

2. she

she

3. he

he

4. wings

wings

5. ears

ears

6. eyes

eyes

82

⊙ Circle the correct word for each sentence.

1.

The boy (**is**, **has**) Tom.

2.

He (**is**, **has**) John.

3.

The girl (**is**, **has**) Jane.

4.

She (**is**, **has**) Julie.

83

Choose and write.

eyes　　ears　　mouth　　wings

1. 　　It has big __eyes__ .

2. 　　It has a big **mouth** .

3. 　　It has two **wings** .

4. 　　It has long _ears_ .

83

3 I Am Running

A Read and write.

1.

walk   run

walk   run

2.

fly   swim

fly   swim

3.

sing   dance

sing   dance

4.

cook   eat

cook   eat

84

B Match and write.

1. walking **walking**

2. running **running**

3. flying **flying**

4. swimming **swimming**

5. singing **singing**

6. dancing **dancing**

84

Circle the correct word for each sentence.

1.

I am (**walking**, running).

2.

I am (**walking**, running).

3.

I am (**swimming**, flying).

4.

I am (**swimming**, flying).

85

D Choose and write.

eating	dancing	cooking	singing

1.

The girl is __singing__ .

2.

The boy is __dancing__ .

3.

Mom is __cooking__ .

4.

Tom is __eating__ .

85

You Are Sleeping

 Read and write.

1.

I you we

I you we

2.

he she they

he she they

86

Match and write.

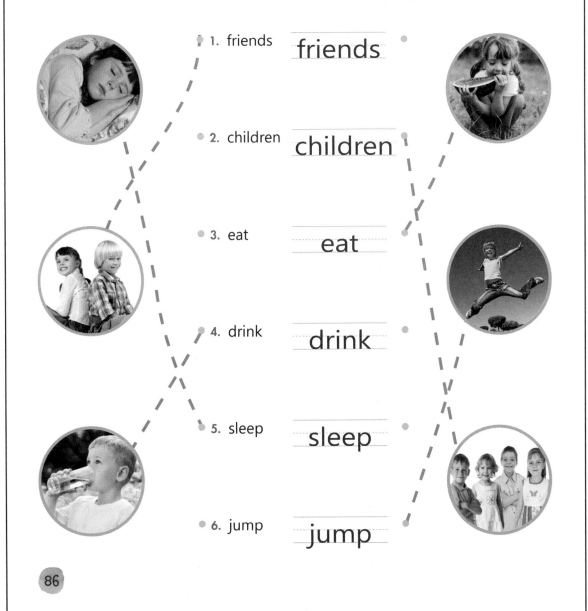

1. friends   friends
2. children   children
3. eat   eat
4. drink   drink
5. sleep   sleep
6. jump   jump

Circle the correct word for each sentence.

1.

I (**am**, **are**) Ann.

2.

You (**am**, **are**) Tom.

3.

We (**is**, **are**) friends.

4.

They (**is**, **are**) children.

5.

He (**is**, **are**) a boy.

6.

She (**is**, **are**) a girl.

87

D Choose and write.

> jumping   eating   drinking   sleeping

1.

I am __eating__ pizza.

2.

You are __drinking__ milk.

3.

We are __jumping__ together.

4.

They are __sleeping__.

87

5 I Run

A Read and write.

1.

rabbit

rabbit

2.

turtle

turtle

3.

frog

frog

4.

dolphin

dolphin

88

B Match and write.

1. I run.

   I run.

2. You walk.

   You walk.

3. We jump.

   We jump.

4. They swim.

   They swim.

ⓒ Circle the correct word for each sentence.

1.

I am a rabbit.
I (**run**, **swim**) fast.

2.

You are a turtle.
You (**walk**, **sing**) slowly.

3.

We are frogs.
We (**jump**, **sing**) well.

4.

They are dolphins.
They (**swim**, **run**) well.

89

D Choose and write.

sing	run	like	swim

1.

   I __like__ to dance.
   I dance well.

2.

   I like to sing.
   I __sing__ well.

3.

   I like to run.
   I __run__ fast.

4.

   I like to swim.
   I __swim__ well.

89

Daily Test 6 — She Runs

A Read and write.

1.

she

she

he

he

it

it

2.

She runs.

She runs.

It sings.

It sings.

90

B Match and write.

1. She sings well.

   She sings well.

2. He dances well.

   He dances well.

3. It swims fast.

   It swims fast.

4. It runs fast.

   It runs fast.

90

C Circle the correct word for each sentence.

1.
I see a girl.
She (**sing,** **sings**) well.

2.
I see a boy.
He (**dance,** **dances**) well.

3.
I see a fish.
It (**swim,** **swims**) fast.

4.
I see a horse.
It (**run,** **runs**) fast.

91

D Choose and write.

likes   eats   jumps   dances

1. He **likes** to run.
   He runs fast.

2. He likes to jump.
   He **jumps** well.

3. He likes to dance.
   He **dances** well.

4. He likes to eat.
   He **eats** well.

91

7 Go, Went

A Read and write.

1.

school

school

2.

park

park

3.

movie

movie

4.

party

party

92

B Match and write.

1. come home

come home

2. go to school

go to school

3. do homework

do homework

4. play baseball

play baseball

5. see a bird

see a bird

6. eat an apple

eat an apple

Circle the correct word for each sentence.

1.

   Yesterday, I (**go, went**) to school.

2.

   Yesterday, I (**come, came**) home early.

3.

   Yesterday, I (**eat, ate**) an apple.

4.

   Yesterday, I (**do, did**) my homework.

5.

   Yesterday, I (**see, saw**) a bird.

6.

   Yesterday, I (**play, played**) baseball.

93

D Choose and write.

went to	saw	played	ate

1.

Yesterday, I __saw__ a bird.
I __played__ baseball.

2.

Yesterday, I __went to__ a party.
I __ate__ cake.

93

Daily Test 8
Will, Be Going to

A Read and write.

1.

soccer

soccer

2.

baseball

baseball

3.

bike

bike

4.

birthday

birthday

94

B Match and write.

1. play soccer

play soccer

2. play a game

play a game

3. play with friends

play with friends

4. ride a bike

ride a bike

5. watch TV

watch TV

6. have a party

have a party

94

ⓒ Circle the correct word for each sentence.

1.

Tomorrow, I will (**play,** **played**) soccer.

2.

Tomorrow, you will (**go,** **went**) to school.

3.

Tomorrow, I am (**go,** **going**) to go to the park.

4.

Tomorrow, you are going to (**play,** **played**) a game.

95

D **Choose and write.**

> eat   have   come   going to   play

1. Tomorrow, I will __**have**__ a party.

2. My friends will __**come**__ to my party.

3. We are __**going to**__ eat cake.

4. We are going to __**eat**__ pizza.

5. We are going to __**play**__ a game.

95